WELSH HISTORY ST

ERDDIG
THE SERVANTS' DAY

JOHN EVANS

Illustrated by Clive Spong

DREF WEN

This is Squire Yorke and his family.
It is the summer of 1912, and they are relaxing in the garden of their home at Erddig as their servants work around them.

Every morning at five o'clock Edith the maid is at work, lighting the fire in the kitchen. Mrs Williams, the cook, begins to prepare the breakfast for the Squire and his family.

Miss Brown the housekeeper, stern and cross, enters the kitchen to check on the work. The keys hanging from her waist jingle and clink. Then she goes to write out the menus for the Squire's dinner-party tonight.

At seven o'clock, John the footman hears the Squire's bell ring. He takes the jug of hot water to the Squire's bedroom, so that he can wash. John says "Good morning, sir", and brings down his master's chamber pot to empty.

By nine o'clock, the family have finished their breakfast. Miss Hitchman, the governess, walks importantly up the stairs. She is on her way to the nursery for today's lesson with Philip and Simon, the Squire's sons. Without a word, Miss Hitchman passes Mary, the chambermaid, who is busy brushing the stairs.

At eleven o'clock, Alice and Mary are busy at work in the laundry. Alice enjoys singing as she scrubs the clothes clean in the wash-tub.

Mary turns the handle of the mangle to squeeze the water out of the wet sheets, and wipes her sweating brow.

Edith clears the lunch away in the dining-room, while in the stable-yard John Jones is polishing the carriage. It has to be ready for the mistress to take her afternoon drive to Wrexham.

John is proud of the gleaming carriage and the well-groomed horse. His master talks of buying a motor car, but John does not like these new-fangled inventions.

The clock chimes in the Butler's Pantry as William uncorks the wine for tonight's dinner. He likes to take just a small sip to make sure that it is of the best quality. Then he must give the footmen their orders for this evening.

Albert, the head gardener, enters the kitchen with the vegetables for tonight's dinner. He checks the time on his pocket-watch with the clock in the kitchen. "Don't bring your dirty boots into my nice clean kitchen!" screams Mrs Williams. Albert is hoping for a mug of tea, but Mrs Williams is far too busy to bother with him today.

The guests begin to arrive at seven o'clock. John, the footman, greets them in the entrance hall and shows them to the saloon. Frank, the other footman serves sherry on a silver tray.

Below stairs, Mrs Williams and her maids are busy in the sweltering kitchen.

The dinner-plates are being washed. Poor Edith! She has broken a tea-cup and is scolded by Miss Brown for being so clumsy.

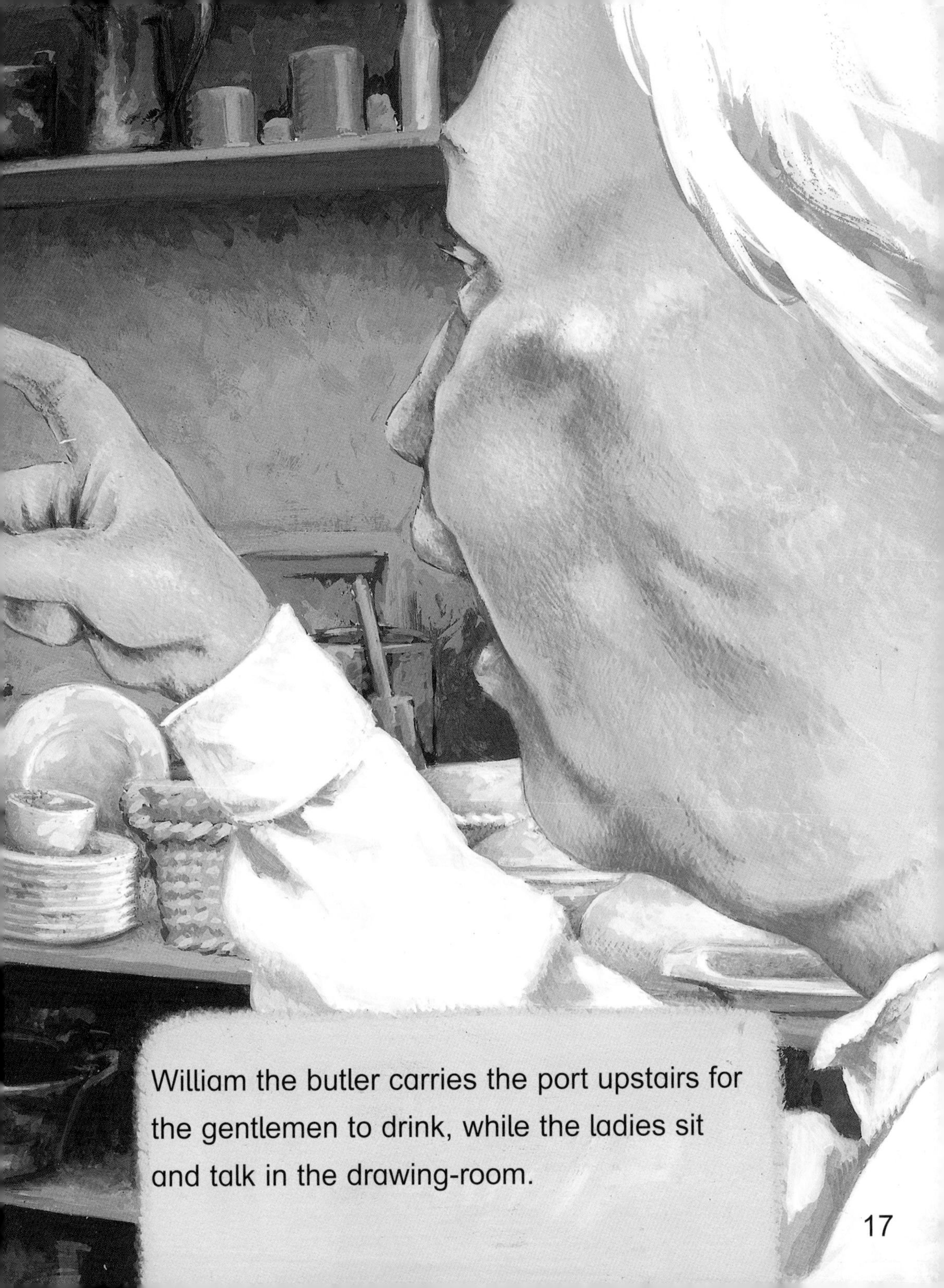

William the butler carries the port upstairs for the gentlemen to drink, while the ladies sit and talk in the drawing-room.

By eleven o'clock, the last dishes have been washed and put away. Miss Brown has locked the pantry door and sent the maids to bed. William dismisses the footmen and now sits down to enjoy a cup of cocoa and a gossip with Miss Brown.

In her bed, Edith falls asleep knowing that it will soon be morning, when her work will begin once more.

INDEX

Albert 13
Alice 8

butler 12, 17

carriage 10, 11
chambermaid 7
chamber pot 6
cook 4

dining-room 10
dinner 5, 13

Edith 4, 10, 16, 19

Frank 14
footman 6, 12, 14

John 6, 14
John Jones 10, 11

kitchen 4, 5, 13, 15

laundry 8

Mary 7, 8, 9
Miss Brown 5, 16, 18
Miss Hitchman 7
Mrs Williams 4, 13, 15

Philip 7

squire 3, 4, 5, 6, 7

William 12, 17, 18

 Published by Gwasg y Dref Wen, 28 Church Road, Whitchurch, Cardiff CF14 2EA. Telephone 029 20617860. Printed in Thailand.
Cover design: Elgan Davies. Back cover illustration: Servants bells at Erddig © National Trust Photographic Library/Andreas von Einsiedel
With thanks to Erddig, a National Trust property.